First Facts™

Holidays and Culture

Cinco de Mayo

Day of Mexican Pride

by **Amanda Doering**

Consultant:
Colin M. MacLachlan
John Christy Barr Distinguished Professor of History
Tulane University
New Orleans, Louisiana

Capstone *press*
Mankato, Minnesota

First Facts is published by Capstone Press,
151 Good Counsel Drive, P.O. Box 669, Mankato, Minnesota 56002.
www.capstonepress.com

Library of Congress Cataloging-in-Publication Data
Doering, Amanda.
    Cinco de Mayo : day of Mexican pride / by Amanda Doering.
    p. cm.—(First facts. Holidays and culture)
    Summary: "A brief description of what Cinco de Mayo is, how it started, and ways people
celebrate this cultural holiday"—Provided by publisher.
    Includes bibliographical references and index.
    ISBN-13: 978-0-7368-5387-3 (hardcover)
    ISBN-10: 0-7368-5387-1 (hardcover)
    1. Cinco de Mayo (Mexican holiday)—History—Juvenile literature. 2. Mexico—Social life
and customs—Juvenile literature. I. Title. II. Series.
F1233.D65 2006
394.262—dc22   2005015587

Editorial Credits
Jennifer Besel, editor; Juliette Peters, designer; Wanda Winch, photo researcher; Scott Thoms,
    photo editor

Photo Credits
Art Directors/Martin Barlow, 4–5
Capstone Press/Karon Dubke, 21
Corbis, 11; Nik Wheeler, 12; Reuters/Andrew Winning, 13; Richard Cummins, 7; Ron Sachs, 20
The Granger Collection, New York, 8
Houserstock/Dave G. Houser, 16
The Image Works/Bob Daemmrich, 14; Kathy McLaughlin, cover
PhotoEdit Inc./Bob Daemmrich, 17; David Young-Wolff, 15, 18
Woodfin Camp & Associates, Inc./Catherine Karnow, 1, 6

1 2 3 4 5 6 11 10 09 08 07 06

Table of Contents

4

Celebrating Cinco de Mayo

A crowd cheers as a parade passes by. **Mariachi** music fills the air. Women spin their colorful dresses to the music, and children wave Mexican flags.

Cinco de Mayo (SEENK-oh DAY MY-oh) is a time to celebrate Mexican history and **culture**. Families take time to honor their way of life.

Fact!

Cinco de Mayo is Spanish for "fifth of May."

5

What Is Cinco de Mayo?

Each year on May 5, Mexicans celebrate a great victory. They remember soldiers who won a battle against all odds.

For Mexican Americans, Cinco de Mayo is a time to celebrate the Mexican way of life. Their fun celebrations showcase many Mexican **customs**.

Battle of Puebla

In the 1800s, Mexico's government borrowed money from France. By 1862, the French wanted their money, but Mexico couldn't pay it back yet. So, France sent its army to take control of the country. The French attacked the city of Puebla.

The small but brave Mexican army fought back. The French had better weapons, but the Mexican soldiers won the battle.

A New Holiday

The Mexican people were very proud of the victory over the French. They began to gather every year to honor Mexican soldiers.

Mexican Americans in California were also proud. To honor their **heritage**, they held Cinco de Mayo dances. Today, these celebrations have grown and spread throughout the United States.

Fact!

Cinco de Mayo is not Mexico's Independence Day. Mexicans celebrate their independence on September 16.

Celebrating in Mexico

Today, Puebla holds a big celebration to remember the victory. Long parades honor soldiers and Mexican history. People eat, dance, and sing together on this special day.

In Mexico City, people act out the Battle of Puebla. They dress in old uniforms and carry old-fashioned weapons. History comes alive for the crowd.

Celebrating in the United States

Mexican Americans have their own ways of celebrating Cinco de Mayo. Parade marchers wear traditional clothing as they walk or ride down the street.

At parties, food, music, and dance
honor the Mexican way of life. People
eat tacos and other traditional foods as
they enjoy the fun events of the day.

Music and Dancing

On Cinco de Mayo, mariachi bands thrill crowds with their lively music. Band members wear traditional *charro*, or Mexican cowboy, suits.

Music leads to dancing! In the Mexican hat dance, a man throws his **sombrero** on the ground. His partner dances around the hat.

Piñata Game

Breaking a piñata filled with candy has been a Mexican tradition for hundreds of years. Playing the game is a fun way for children to celebrate their heritage.

Cinco de Mayo is a holiday rich with history. Each tradition is a special way to remember the past and to honor the Mexican culture.

Amazing Holiday Story!

President George W. Bush was the first president to celebrate Cinco de Mayo at the White House. In 2001, he invited many Mexicans and Mexican Americans to a Cinco de Mayo celebration. President Bush gave a speech to honor all that Mexican Americans have done for the United States.

Hands On: Paper Bag Piñata

Piñatas are part of many Cinco de Mayo celebrations. Have an adult help you make and hang this paper bag piñata.

What You Need

a large paper bag
candy
stapler
paper punch
markers
colored tissue paper

crepe paper streamers
other decorations
a long piece of string
blindfold
wooden stick or
    plastic bat

What You Do

1. Fill the paper bag half full of candy.
2. Fold the top of the bag down and staple it shut.
3. Punch two holes on the top of the bag. They should be about 3 inches (8 centimeters) in on both sides.
4. Decorate your piñata with markers, tissue paper, crepe paper streamers, or other decorations.
5. Tie the string through the two holes at the top. Have an adult use the string to hang your piñata from a tree or the ceiling.
6. Blindfold a friend and spin him or her around. Then have your friend try to hit the piñata with the stick. Take turns trying to break the bag.
7. When the piñata breaks, share the candy with everyone.

Glossary

culture (KUHL-chur)—a people's way of life, ideas, art, customs, and traditions

custom (KUHSS-tuhm)—a tradition in a culture or society

heritage (HER-uh-tij)—traditions handed down from the past

mariachi (mar-ee-AH-chee)—a Mexican street band

sombrero (sohm-BRER-oh)—a tall straw or felt hat with a wide brim

Read More

Flanagan, Alice K. *Cinco de Mayo.* Holidays and Festivals. Minneapolis: Compass Point Books, 2004.

Walsh, Kieran. *Cinco de Mayo: Holiday Celebrations.* Vero Beach, Fla.: Rourke, 2003.

Internet Sites

FactHound offers a safe, fun way to find Internet sites related to this book. All of the sites on FactHound have been researched by our staff.

Here's how:
1. Visit *www.facthound.com*
2. Type in this special code **0736853871** for age-appropriate sites. Or enter a search word related to this book for a more general search.
3. Click on the **Fetch It** button.

FactHound will fetch the best sites for you!

Index